EARLY WORLD CIVILIZATIONS
2nd Grade History Book
Children's Ancient History Edition

Speedy Publishing LLC
40 E. Main St. #1156
Newark, DE 19711
www.speedypublishing.com

The modern day
cultures and
civilizations owe
a lot to the first
of the civilization
that originated
after millions of
years of evolution
in human history.

Ancient Mesopotamia refers to the place where humans first formed civilizations.

It was here that people first gathered in large cities, learned to write, and created governments.

Widely considered
to be the one of the
cradles of civilization
by the Western
world, Bronze Age
Mesopotamia included
Sumer and the
Akkadian, Babylonian,
and Assyrian empires.

The heart of Mesopotamia lies between the two rivers in southern Iraq. The land on the sides of the rivers was fertile while the general area was not and this led to irrigation techniques.

Mosul
Aleppo
Latakia
Euphrates
Khābūr
MESOPO
Tharthār Depression
SYRIA
Damascus
Sea of Galilee
Beirut
NON
SYRIAN
IRA
Bahr al Mil
Bac
Jabal 'Unayzah
Ammān
DESERT
Wadi
5905
3068
3510
1385
1381
3675
Ur

4180
Qezel
Owzan
Teheran
Asadābād Pass
11073
7241
Namak
Lake
S
Z
a
Diyala
g
r
o
Dez
Qom
R
P
E
R
Karkheh
s
Isfah
Zard Kūh
14921
Q
O
4100
M
I
A
Karūn
M
o
Euphrates
Hawr al
Hammār
Shatt al
Basra
Arab
Būb
Şahrā' al Hijārat
1212

Mesopotamians developed glass, the Pythagorean Theorem, and ancient sanitation techniques.

Mesopotamians invented the wheel in approximately 3500 BC.

Ancient Egypt was a civilization of ancient Northeastern Africa, concentrated along the lower reaches of the Nile River in what is now the modern country of Egypt.

Ancient Egypt was one of the greatest and most powerful civilizations in the history of the world.

The Nile was the source of much of the Ancient Egypt's wealth.

The Nile provided
food, soil, water,
and transportation
for the Egyptians.

They were one of
the first civilizations
to invent writing.
They also used ink
to write and paper
called papyrus.

Religion played
a big part in the
lives of the Ancient
Egyptians. The Ancient
Egyptians considered
Pharaoh to be their
main intermediary
to the gods.

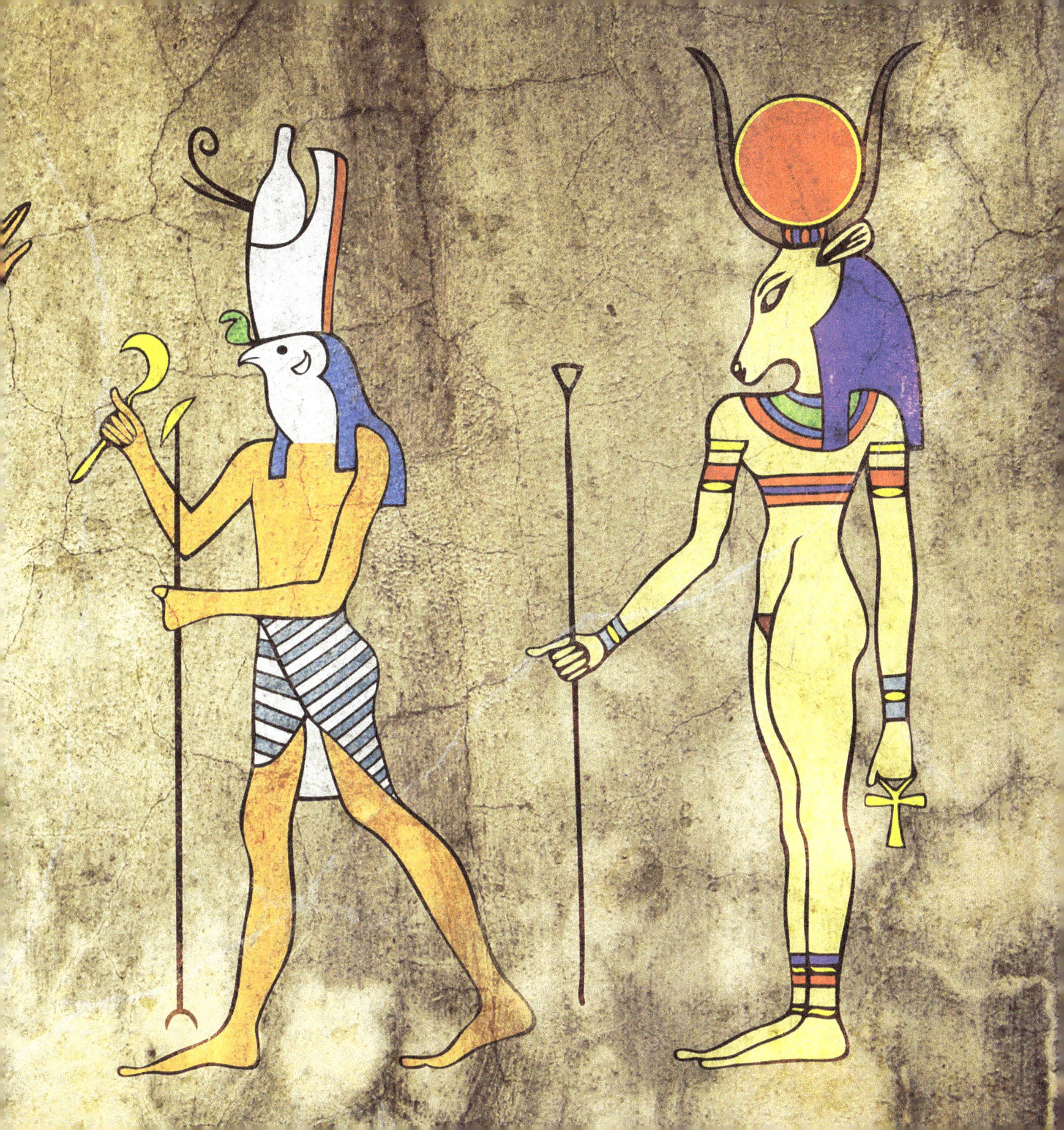

**Ancient Greece
was a civilization
belonging to a period
of Greek history.**

The earliest Greek
civilizations thrived
nearly 4,000 years ago.

The Greeks were
the first to have
a democratic
government. They lived
in city-states. Each
city-state had its own
laws and government.

Athens and Sparta
were the two main city
states that ruled much
of ancient Greece.

The Ancient
Greeks played an
important part in
the development of
the alphabet. The
Greeks made many
advancements in
the areas of science
and technology.

The ancient Greeks
were polytheastic,
which means they
had many gods and
goddesses. Zeus was
the king of the Greek
gods who lived on
Mount Olympus.

MAXIM

MMIV
OPILIVS

Visit
BABY PROFESSOR
EDUCATION KIDS
www.BabyProfessorBooks.com
to download Free Baby Professor eBooks
and view our catalog of new and exciting
Children's Books